What Is the Trinity

and Why Does It Matter?

THE JESUS WAY
—SMALL BOOKS *of* RADICAL FAITH—

What Is the Trinity

and Why Does It Matter?

STEVE DANCAUSE

HERALD
P R E S S

Harrisonburg, Virginia

Herald Press
PO Box 866, Harrisonburg, Virginia 22803
www.HeraldPress.com

Library of Congress Cataloging-in-Publication Data
Names: Dancause, Steve, author.
Title: What is the trinity and why does it matter? / Steve Dancause.
Description: Harrisonburg, Virginia : Herald Press, 2020. | Series: The
 Jesus way: small books of radical faith | Includes bibliographical
 references.
Identifiers: LCCN 2019049747 (print) | LCCN 2019049748 (ebook) | ISBN
 9781513805689 (paperback) | ISBN 9781513806174 (ebook)
Subjects: LCSH: Trinity.
Classification: LCC BT111.3 .D36 2020 (print) | LCC BT111.3 (ebook) | DDC
 231/.044--dc23
LC record available at https://lccn.loc.gov/2019049747
LC ebook record available at https://lccn.loc.gov/2019049748

WHAT IS THE TRINITY AND WHY DOES IT MATTER?
© 2020 by Herald Press, Harrisonburg, Virginia 22803. 800-245-7894.
    All rights reserved.
Library of Congress Control Number: 2019049747
International Standard Book Number: 978-1-5138-0568-9 (paperback);
    978-1-5138-0617-4 (ebook)
Printed in United States of America
Cover and interior design by Reuben Graham

24 23 22 21 20   10 9 8 7 6 5 4 3 2 1

Contents

Introduction to The Jesus Way Series from Herald Press

The Jesus Way is good news for all people, of all times, in all places. Jesus Christ "is before all things, and in him all things hold together"; "in him all the fullness of God was pleased to dwell" (Colossians 1:17, 19). The Jesus Way happens when God's will is done on earth as it is in heaven.

But what does it mean to walk the Jesus Way? How can we who claim the name of Christ reflect the image of God in the twenty-first century? What does it mean to live out and proclaim the good news of reconciliation in Christ?

The Jesus Way: Small Books of Radical Faith offers concise, practical theology that helps readers encounter big questions about God's work in the world. Grounded in a Christ-centered reading of Scripture and a commitment to reconciliation, the series aims to enliven the service and embolden the witness of people who follow Jesus. The volumes in the series are written by a diverse community of internationally renowned pastors, scholars, and practitioners committed to the way of Jesus.

The Jesus Way series is rooted in Anabaptism, a Christian tradition that prioritizes following Jesus, loving enemies, and creating faithful communities. During the Protestant Reformation of the 1500s, early Anabaptists who began meeting for worship emphasized discipleship in addition to belief, baptized adults instead of infants, and pledged their allegiance to God over loyalty to the state. Early Anabaptists were martyred for their radical faith, and they went to their deaths without violently resisting their accusers.

Today more than two million Anabaptist Christians worship in more than one hundred countries around the globe. They include Mennonites, Amish, Brethren in Christ, and Hutterites. Many other Christians committed to Anabaptist beliefs and practices remain in church communities in other traditions.

Following Jesus means turning from sin, renouncing violence, seeking justice, believing in the reconciling power of God, and living in the power of the Holy Spirit. The Jesus Way liberates us from conformity to the world and heals broken places. It shines light on evil and restores all things.

Join Christ-followers around the world as we seek the Jesus Way.

Introduction

We all build on foundations. Jesus teaches that this is true with buildings, and true of our faith as well. In 2007, my good friends Tom and Ally bought their first house. Of course they were full of excitement, and it seemed that God wanted to bless them with this home. Six months later, they found out that the foundation was cracked and failing. It would cost a lot to fix. They could avoid fixing it, but it would slowly destroy the house. Any repairs or remodeling done to such a house would be wasted if they did not first fix the foundation, as problems would keep coming back. Just as Tom and Ally hired a contractor to begin repairs, the financial crisis of 2008 hit, and soon they were deep underwater on their mortgage. They struggled and wondered why God would put them in such a bad position. Over time, they learned a difficult yet valuable lesson; their faith—their view of God—was a bit like their house. It was built on a cracked foundation.

When we build on solid rock, our faith can withstand the storms of life. Our faith foundation is who we trust that God is, no matter our circumstances. Upon this foundation we will frame who Jesus is, who we are, and who we are in relation to God and others. In this volume of The Jesus Way series, we will see how the Trinity is foundational to faith in Jesus. When our foundation is anything else, we inflict a lot of avoidable damage on the life we build. You see, if our foundation is shoddy, then nothing built on it will be level, plumb, or square. The effort and skill put into later construction will be wasted.

A foundation is largely unseen, yet it is the most important part of a structure. From our view of who God is, all other Christian doctrines flow. I admit that the Trinity is scandalous and paradoxical. It is the source of scorn from non-Christians, and a source of bewilderment for some Jesus-followers. The history of Christian theology can be summarized by countless movements to dilute the Trinity, attempting to harmonize Christianity with many other world religions. Yet among all the tenets of the Christian faith, the Trinity is unique. There are Buddhists who believe in salvation by grace through faith alone. Muslims believe in eternal life. Hindus believe in the greatness of Jesus. Jehovah's Witnesses believe in Christ's atoning sacrifice on the cross, and Mormons believe in the resurrection of Jesus.[1] While all these doctrines are essential, only belief in the Trinity makes Christianity distinct from other worldviews.

Let that sink in. Anyone can believe in God. Anyone can believe in Jesus. Even some atheists believe in Jesus and a god-like ultimate power that they call the universe. So who or what is this God that we are talking about? For Christ-followers, the God we should be talking about is the Trinity. It is the one thing that distinguishes Christianity, and it is the one God that Jesus reveals.

When we build on *this* foundation, the other doctrines find their anchor. The sureness of a foundation is apparent with the test of time. Over time, the Trinity has set Christianity apart from every worldview imaginable. It demonstrates that God is sacrificial, personal love. Love requires a community of persons, freely giving and receiving life. God has always been this community of love, and always will be. This love has been clearly revealed to us in and through Jesus Christ. God's gift of eternal life is the extension of this love to us. In this volume we will explore the tapestry of Scripture, history, and theology that makes faith in the Trinity compelling. Throughout the book, key terms appear in bold and are defined in the glossary.

This book comprises seven chapters, each of which answers an important question:

1. What does faith in the Trinity look like?
2. Why do Christians believe in the Trinity?
3. Is our image of God individual or communal?
4. Why does Jesus, above all else, reveal God to us?
5. How is God perfectly one, yet perfectly three?
6. Why isn't the Father alone really God?
7. What does the Trinity say about gender, hierarchy, and roles?

And within these chapters we will explore other questions as well: How are Jesus and the Holy Spirit equal to the Father? How is Jesus fully God and fully human? Who in the world should we pray to? And why in the world does any of it matter?

It matters because the walls of our churches are cracking all around us. Pipes are breaking, flooding our homes. The roofs of human society are at risk of caving in. We can keep patching things up, but it is better to go to the foundation and do the hard digging. With the right foundation, the structure holds, and it stands the test of eternity. The Trinity is a foundation that we can build our lives on each and every day. And it is only in Jesus, and the Trinity he reveals to us, that we build our lives on solid rock.

Let's dig down together.

1

What Does Faith in the Trinity Look Like?

I pray that, according to the riches of [the Father's] glory, he may grant that you may be strengthened in your inner being with power through his Spirit, and that Christ may dwell in your hearts through faith, as you are being rooted and grounded in love.
—Ephesians 3:16-17

At my previous church in Pennsylvania, a young man named Scott came to me for advice. He was married with two kids, and was struggling to be a good husband and father. The "in love" phase of his marriage had faded away, and he had trouble finding meaning and enjoyment in being a father. I could relate. Scott also had theological objections to our church's position on nonviolence and peace. He was a devout Christian, but Jesus' example was not quite enough for him.

He wasn't willing to value the revelation of Jesus above violent depictions of God he found in the Old Testament. Scott's personal struggles and his theological objections seemed to be unrelated, but we soon found out that they both were built on the same cracked foundation.

Jesus teaches that there is only one eternal foundation—the God of love who is the Trinity. We resist building our lives on this foundation because it requires that we be rooted and grounded in love, and nothing else. Yet when we consent to a life ruled by this love, we find that God does the hard work for us when we cannot. Faith in Jesus holds a radical premise: the same God who created the universe has dwelt among us in the person of Jesus. And this same God indwells us now in the person of the Holy Spirit, empowering us to be transformed into the likeness of Jesus. Of course, we can always choose against growth and maturity in Christ.

We can cut ourselves off at the knees by not believing that the Spirit within us is fully God. This is tragic, as we presently have everything that we need to grow toward God. What do we have? We have God—God as a human in the person of Jesus, and God within and between us in the person of the Holy Spirit. Christianity is built on believing that Jesus is fully God (John 1; Philippians 2), and that Jesus is the exact representation of God's being to us (Hebrews 1). Without these truths, we end up with an unlovable, distant Father, and a Son and Spirit who aren't God after all. Our Christianity literally becomes *Godless*.

This matters for our daily lives. Christian discipleship is learning to practice the way of Jesus in order to become more like Jesus. Most Christians say that they believe in the Trinity, but true belief involves behaving as if our convictions are true. True faith is lived out in our behavior, in what we practice daily. Right now, I need to grow in having patience with my daughter. I love her, but she drives me crazy, and as her father I am not always my best self. Yet if part of me thinks I need not imitate Jesus, or if I fear that the Spirit within me is unable to empower me to parent better, then the fruit of the Spirit I need to be a better father is not going to grow.

If we don't believe that Jesus is fully God, then we aren't likely to obey his teaching when it isn't convenient, nor are we likely to accept him as God's ultimate revelation. Instead of Jesus being the exact representation of God's being, he becomes just one friendly version of God among other versions we can choose from. Those who are not Jesus-followers are free to choose what they believe about Jesus and live accordingly, but it is alarming that so many Christians do the same. We can choose the cultural god of the time, or can choose isolated and out-of-context depictions of a violent Old Testament God, over the revelation of God in Jesus Christ. This seems logical—we are using Scripture after all, and the Father alone is really God, right?

Wrong. This thinking lends credence to squirming out of the commands of Jesus that we don't like. Jesus is seen as merely the Son of God, but not really God. Turn the other cheek? Sounds nice, but the Father didn't command that in the Old Testament, so Jesus must mean something else. When the reality of the Trinity is not taken seriously, we lose the primacy of Jesus. We end up turning the Bible on its head and use it to promote violence instead of love, bad news instead of good news. This results in all the horrors of church history with which we are all too familiar. Without the Trinity—in which all three persons are equally God and where Jesus is the exact representation of God's character to us—the entire house comes crashing down.

A low view of the Holy Spirit is similarly detrimental. If we do not see the Spirit as fully God, then we aren't likely to believe that our lives can be radically transformed. It takes God within us to deliver us from sin and free us from fear. It takes the Spirit of Jesus in us to empower us to follow the narrow way of Jesus. When we don't believe that the Spirit in us is fully God, then we have not only a low view of God, but also a low view of ourselves and what God can do in and through us. When we view the Spirit as less than fully God, the Bible's talk about our transformation need not be taken literally.

This is the reason I ended up sitting across the table from Scott talking about the Trinity. It's the root cause of a lot of lives that are crumbling with despair and meaninglessness. *When we don't believe in the Trinity, we don't believe deep down that the Jesus Way is something that is doable.* Scott had come to this conclusion. He thought that the commands of Jesus to love our enemies are simply impossible and unwise given human nature. Jesus might embody the heavenly ideal, but not the worldly real. Yet with a higher view of the Trinity, the ideal becomes real. The work of the church is to be this visible reality for the world. Our lives should demonstrate that against all odds, love prevails. Against all the storms of the world, God saves and restores.

In John 14, Jesus says that the way to love God is to obey Jesus' commands, and the way to obey Jesus' commands is to love God and each other. Love and life go hand in hand. When we fail to love, we fail to believe in the Trinity who *is* love. This love is self-giving and self-sacrificing. It puts others first, and it is perfectly revealed in Jesus, not the veiled and "shadowy" representations of God we find in the Old Covenant (see Colossians 2:17; Hebrews 10:1). Jesus said that the world would know his disciples by our love for one another.

We need to let Jesus define what this love looks like, and the Trinity is essential to his definition.

Scott's concerns were about Bible interpretation, politics, and power. After a few meetings I asked him, "What would your faith look like if you had as high a view of Jesus and the Spirit as you do of the Father alone?" Scott was stunned. He had never wrestled with how the Trinity matters. Most of us have not, but it affects our thinking on the Bible, on politics, and on our everyday relationships.

Scott discovered that squirming out of certain teachings of Jesus that he didn't like was not serving his marriage well. God was calling him to sacrificial love. Believing that he *should* do this required that he adopt a higher view of Jesus as Lord and God. Acting as if he *could* embody sacrificial love required that he adopt a higher view of the Spirit as God within him. It was hard, but Scott decided that it was worth it. It took some time, and Scott said that it often felt like death. He was learning to lose his life to find it.

You see, a foundation does not merely exist in and for itself. It holds a structure up even while it keeps the structure anchored to the ground. Establishing a lasting foundation is absolutely necessary, but it is hard work, and building on it can feel limiting. We protest, "But I want to build on this today, and on that tomorrow! Or perhaps I want to build on nothing at all. Don't tie me down!"

Faith in the Trinity is a foundation on which we can build endlessly. To imagine your life built on this love, it helps to spend time with God through prayer, community, and Scripture. And it would help to read the other nine books in this Jesus Way series to learn about the necessary tools and supplies that Jesus, our master builder, gives us. Yet it all comes down to love. The word *love* is cliché, abused, and overused in our culture. We use it to sell stuff that we think will make us happy. Only real life—a life of meaning, a life that lasts, a life with God and others, a life that is filled and poured out for others and filled again—will bring us lasting joy. This is life in the Trinity, and Jesus shows us the way.

2

Why Do Christians Believe in the Trinity?

All authority in heaven and on earth has been given to me. Go therefore and make disciples of all nations, baptizing them in the name of the Father and of the Son and of the Holy Spirit, and teaching them to obey everything that I have commanded you. And remember, I am with you always, to the end of the age.
—Matthew 28:18-20

Let's start surveying the ground of our foundation by reviewing the history that gave us belief in the Trinity. It is a long story, and we would need a book three feet thick to tell it in detail. Perhaps you won't mind if I summarize: In the Old Testament witness, God revealed Godself to the nation of Israel as one. These people, who were surrounded by cultures who worshiped many different gods, experienced

God as one, and they found this experience to be compelling. Then, in Jesus, something new happened. This same God of all things was revealed as God in three persons—Father, Son, and Holy Spirit. The followers of Jesus experienced God as three, and they found this experience to be radically life altering. Yet it isn't that the God of the Old Covenant was wrong, it is that the revelation of the Old Covenant wasn't complete. Jesus revealed that the one is the three and the three are the one. This was the witness of the first followers of Jesus, and of Christians ever since.

Christians often tell me that the Trinity is not a contradiction, but it certainly appears that way on the surface. This is because the Trinity is a **paradox**, which is when two ideas contradict each other but are both found to be true anyway. When this happens, something deep is usually at play. Writer G. K. Chesterton is credited with saying, "Paradox is truth standing on its head to get attention." If someone came up to you walking on their hands with their feet in the air, you might be annoyed or concerned, but you would certainly notice. Paradoxes demand and deserve our attention. Currently, the imagination of many scientists is captured by the paradox of quantum theory versus the theory of general relativity. Both have been shown to be absolutely true, yet each suggests that the other must be false. So scientists are searching for the deeper truth that makes both theories true. Who knows what they might find. In this book, I hope that you will let your imagination be captured by the deep truth of the Trinity.

The first Christians believed in the Trinity because it was their experience, and it was the faith and revelation of Jesus himself. It was not something the church invented. The early church leaders did not argue for the Trinity simply to win an intellectual battle. They saw that our salvation was dependent on the full divinity of the Son and Spirit. Only God can save us. If our Savior is not really God, how can we be saved? Only God can transform us. If the Spirit within us is not really God, how can we be transformed? All three divine persons must be fully God for Jesus to be worth following. And all three must be fully God for them to truly be one, and to truly be the one God.

You might be thinking, Why does the Jesus Way require such faith? Christianity would be much more compatible with other worldviews without the Trinity, after all. When we get down to it, we are trinitarian simply because Jesus was trinitarian, as was the witness of his first followers. The Trinity is essential to Jesus' teachings on who he is, as well as to his teachings on how we should live. Without the Trinity and its implication that Jesus Christ and the Spirit are fully God, there is no reason at all to be a Christian. Other religions have everything else that Christianity does.

In fact, without the Trinity, our God-talk about love is meaningless. What grounds our concept of love? Love is used to sell products, but is love really "what makes a Subaru a Subaru"? When we order fast food at McDonald's, do we really "choose lovin"? Like everything we believe, if love is not grounded in the Trinity, then people can take it to mean anything at all, which is the same as meaning nothing at all. The Jesus Way demands that we live in peace with the world, but it certainly does not demand that we live in conformity with the world. Love, as defined by God as Trinity, exemplifies the Jesus Way. It is clearly demonstrated by Christ's sacrifice for us on the cross. Or we can let the world define love—demonstrated by eating chicken nuggets, or whatever else we want it to mean.

At the end of the gospel of Matthew, Jesus gives us the great commission: "All authority in heaven and on earth has been given to me. Go therefore and make disciples of all nations, baptizing them in the name of the Father and of the Son and of the Holy Spirit, and teaching them to obey everything that I have commanded you. And remember, I am with you always, to the end of the age" (Matthew 28:18-20). There is much we can say about this passage, but for now I would like to point us toward this "name" in which Jesus directs us to baptize. Jesus is not so much revealing God's name here as claiming that the God who is beyond naming consists of three persons. Three unique persons who all share one *singular* name.

In the Hebrew Bible we are given many titles for God, but the closest we get to a proper name for God is in Exodus 3, when Moses asks God whom he should say sent him to the Israelites. God answers with "I AM WHO I AM" or "I WILL BE WHAT I WILL BE" (**YHWH** in Hebrew is shorthand for "I am who I am"). God further answers with "'YHWH, the God of your ancestors, the God of Abraham, the God of Isaac, and the God of Jacob has sent me to you.' This is my name forever." God is telling Moses two things. The first is that God's proper name, "I am who I am," is a name that is beyond naming. This name defies being boxed in. The second thing to notice is that God is relational. This God is the God of Abraham, and Isaac, and Jacob. This God is the God *of* people with whom this God is in relationship, people like you and me. While God is beyond capturing with language, we can know God through personal relationship.

In the great commission, Jesus gives us another take on God's name: "The name of the Father and of the Son and of the Holy Spirit." In English it is not clear if this sentence implies one name that three share, or three separate names. However, the original Greek is clear that this name for God is a single name for all three. Jesus does not quite come out and tell us what this name for God is. He simply says that Father, Son, and Spirit all have this one name. God is still beyond human language, and is still known through personal relationship. The additional implication is that God exists in and through the personal relationship among Father, Son, and Spirit. The one is the three, and the three are one.

The first followers of Jesus were Jews who believed in the one God of ancient Israel. Looking back, it is easy for us to see the Trinity in Jewish Scripture, but while their Scriptures sometimes referred to God in the plural, the ancient Israelites understood God to be a single divine person. In short, the Father was Lord and God. For Jews in Jesus' time, to call anyone Lord was equivalent to calling them God. Therefore, to call anyone Lord other than YHWH was blasphemy.

The first Christians had to wrestle with their Jewish belief in the Father along with their experience that Jesus was also Lord and God. Jesus affirmed that God is indeed one, and that God is our Father. Yet Jesus also taught that he himself was one with the Father. His disciples called him Lord, and even God. Jesus plainly taught that he was himself God, even calling himself the equivalent of YHWH in John 8:58. Jesus also claimed authority to do things that only God could do, such as forgive sins. All this is why the religious authorities wanted to kill him. They had good reasons, and they got their wish, but proof of Jesus' divinity came with his bodily resurrection. The letters of the New Testament would further witness to Jesus' full divinity.

The first Christians also had to grapple with their experience of being indwelt by the Holy Spirit. Jesus had taught that he and the Father were one with another person he called the

Spirit. And Jesus promised that through himself, the Father would send them the Spirit, another counselor of the same type as the Father and Son (John 14:16). When the Spirit did come, there was no doubt in their minds that the Spirit was the same God as the Father and Jesus. So the first Christians began calling this Spirit Lord and God, as did the New Testament writers. They were not willing to accept three separate Gods and give up on the one God of Jewish Scripture, nor were they content to keep the single-person God of their Jewish religion. Something new had been revealed in Christ Jesus: God is one being in three persons.

Thomas Finger puts it like this: "In the early church then Spirit, Son, and Father were experienced as salvation's direct agents, sometimes operating in a threefold, interwoven dynamic. This reveals much about relationships among them. It also entails that each one, and altogether, are divine."[1]

Eventually the church would settle on the language that God is *one being in three persons*. The word *Trinity* came to be used for this experience. Yet the early church struggled with what the revelation of God as Trinity implied. People disagreed about whether the Father was greater than the Son and Spirit. And they disagreed on how and whether they could really be one. In the fourth century a man named Arius began teaching that the Son was a created being and therefore not really God. Arius had Greco-Roman philosophy, culture, and plenty of Scripture verses to back him up. This caused a controversy, and forced the church to explicitly state whether or not Jesus really was God and one being with the Father. At the first ecumenical council at Nicaea in the year 325, they decided that Jesus was fully God, and the Trinity was upheld.

The texts that Arius used to prove Jesus' inferiority had been taken out of context. The whole point of Jesus is that he is and was God, but took on the form of a servant. He humbled himself to the point of death on a cross. In all of this, the Son is not eternally less than the Father. The **incarnation**—the Son's taking on human flesh and living and dying as one of us—does not mean that he became less than God, or ever was anything less than God. He simply took on a lesser status during his earthly ministry. This lesser status was temporary and does not correspond to who he is in eternity. Jesus is eternally God.

Nicaea did not solve the Holy Spirit problem, however. It took another council, the second ecumenical council at Constantinople in the year 381, to uphold the full divinity of the Spirit. From these two councils we received the **Nicene Creed** (or the Niceno-Constantinopolitan Creed). Here what is implied in Scripture and in the revelation of God in Jesus Christ was made explicit.

A one-person God can *act* loving if this God creates, but this God can never *be* love. Love would not be *essential* to this God, for this God was not engaged in loving before creation. Love may not be what makes a Subaru a Subaru, but it is what makes God, God. A lonely God can possibly choose to love, but a lonely God can't possibly be love. And that puts the universe on a very shaky foundation.

God must be communal in nature to be love, and to be worthy of our meager love. Love requires a community of persons. A singular, non-triune God cannot, alone, be love. A lone God has no one else to love. This God must create people to even become loving in the first place. Pastor Bruxy Cavey says, "Love exists within and between persons. Love is relational energy. . . . While there may be relationships without love, there will never be love without relationship. In and of himself, God could not be 'love' without some form of relational experience and expression being intrinsic and elemental to who God is."[2]

The Trinity is loving before, during, and after creation, because the Trinity *is* interpersonal love. A single-person God has no reason to become loving and has no way to experience mutual love. If perfect Godliness is a life of lonely solitude, then why would God ever create another being? Any "other" would only ruin the perfection of divine solitude. It's a cold, lonely, look-out-for-yourself universe with a one-person God. Even Christians can promote this worldview, but it describes the world as Satan would like it to be—a world where the foundation of love is replaced with self-centeredness. The Trinity, however, creates the world out of an overflow of interpersonal, freely giving love.

This love is mysterious. It is beyond controlling and boxing in, but we find it in relationship. And in Jesus, who is God among us, we meet the Father beyond us and the Spirit within us. God is more than willing to stand on God's head to get our attention. In fact, on the cross, God has gone a great deal further than that.

3

Is Our Image of God Individual or Communal?

Then God said "Let us make humankind in our image,
according to our likeness. . . ."
So God created humankind in his image,
in the image of God he created them;
male and female he created them.
—Genesis 1:26-27

In Palestine, the Jordan River feeds two large lakes, the Sea of Galilee and the Dead Sea. People in Jesus' time were familiar with these waters. The Sea of Galilee teams with life, while the Dead Sea cannot sustain most forms of life. Both lakes are fed by the same water source. The only difference is that, because of geography, water flows into the Sea of Galilee and then continues to flow out the other side, while water that flows into the Dead Sea has no outlet. Salts, silts, and other pollutants accumulate in the Dead Sea with nowhere to go. Eventually the levels become toxic and choke out most life.

You and I are similar to lakes. Without an inflow and an outflow, we die. We need to pour ourselves out in love, even as we are poured into, being refreshed with new life. I recognize that as a white male, this is easy for me to say. I've been made aware that marginalized or oppressed groups are often forced to pour out their lives on behalf of others, without being filled in return. Forced sacrifice and one-way love is not the life that God desires for us. The love of the Trinity is freely chosen and mutual. To use God to justify the oppression of others is a gross abuse of theology that deeply distorts the image of God we bear.

The verse that opens this chapter shows us that God is an "us," and that God created humanity in God's image to be an "us." The free-flowing and mutual love of the Trinity shows us that life is not a solo sport. This should be obvious to us given how everyone is conceived and born, but it is uncomfortable for many of us to admit that we are all interdependent. We literally get our life from God and from others. In John 4, Jesus told the woman at the well that he was the source of living water. And in John 7, Jesus promised that if anyone comes to him and drinks, from out of them will flow rivers of living water. But for living waters to flow, we need to let go of the god of our age, individualism. I'm still working on it.

I love individualism. It is the bedrock of Western society, but it is a poor foundation. Our society is built on individual expression, individual rights, and individual thoughts and feelings. Our culture worships individualism to the extent that some of our greatest theologians and philosophers literally think of it as the closest thing to God. An individual's thoughts, feelings, and experiences are called a person's *subjectivity*. And because of our obsession with individual subjectivity, we tend to think of God as a solo, divine subjectivity. *The result is that instead of seeing God as three intersubjective persons, we view God as one person with three facets.* This is a common misconception of the Trinity called **modalism**, in which we think of God as one person with three modes (Father, Son, and Spirit).

Eastern Christianity has always maintained that God is three persons in one being. This has helped Eastern Christianity maintain a communal rather than individual emphasis. If you are reading this, however, you are probably a Western Christian who thinks of God less as a community and more as one person with three modes. The problem with modalism is that it implies that Father, Son, and Spirit are just expressions of God, and that the real God is some fourth thing hidden behind the Trinity. In other words, with modalism the Trinity does not reveal anything essential about God, it is just a superficial perception that we have. When we land here, it becomes easy to throw away the Trinity entirely. When we lose the Trinity, we are left with an entirely different God altogether, and we begin to remake God in our own image.

A further problem with viewing God as one person, rather than a community of persons who are one, is that we end up viewing humanity, who is created in God's image, in an overly individualistic way. Our culture teaches that we become our fullest selves either through distinguishing and separating ourselves from each other, or through enmeshing ourselves to another in order to enable that person's individuality. What the Trinity teaches us is that we actually become our unique selves when we can *freely* give our lives for others. And we can become our fullest selves when we live in a context where others *freely* give their lives for us. Father, Son, and Spirit each are their fullest selves as they pour themselves out for each other, and Jesus demonstrated the essence of who God is by pouring out his life for us. The act of giving and receiving love is essential to community, and it is essential to finding your true individuality. Like the one and the three—individuality and community go together.

Essentially, the Jesus Way is about living into this paradoxical love. It is about opening ourselves up to the love of God and of others. It strikes us as counterintuitive, but we open ourselves up to love only as much as we are willing to pour out our lives in love for others. We can let in only what we are willing to freely pour out, and we can freely give only to the extent that we are able to receive. Some of us need to receive more before we can give. Those who have been given plenty need to recognize that and give in return.

In Scripture there are two big metaphors for life—water and breath. We are like containers meant for water. In John 10:10, Jesus said that he *came so that we might have life, and have it abundantly*. In the original Greek language, this "abundance" of life is a picture of overflowing water, of a jar filled to beyond the brim and spilling out. We are meant not only to hold this water of life, but to be conduits for the water of life to flow through.

When Jesus tells the woman at the well about living water, he goes on to explain that it is the Holy Spirit who supplies this water. The Spirit within and among us fills us with life, but we need to pour it out so that we can be continually refreshed. The Spirit is also often thought of as breath. In fact, "breath" is what the Hebrew and Greek words for "spirit" in the Bible (*ruach* and *pneuma*) literally mean. Just as waters need to be refreshed, so our bodies are refreshed with every breath we take. Once we take in a full breath, we cannot take in any more until we breathe it out. If we refuse to release our breath, then bad things happen. Our own selves and our communities are meant to be the living image of God, where life is freely given and received.

We call this image of God the ***imago Dei***. If God is communal, then we are created in God's communal image. If God is a lonely individual, then we are created to be lonely individuals. And sometimes we feel like lonely individuals. Yet this feeling is a result of the fall, of the propensity for us to eat of the tree of the knowledge of good and evil. Adam and Eve's act of reaching for the fruit of the tree symbolized that they would decide for themselves what is true and what is good. Community with God and each other would not come first, just whatever seems good for oneself right now. Instead of finding life through communion with God and others, we think we can find life through self-absorption. The result is sin, separation, and death—just me, myself, and I.

Love and life need to flow through us. This requires openness to sacrifice in the context of a diverse community. Jesus teaches that we find life in something greater than ourselves. God is a communion of interdependent persons united in love, and we are created in God's image to be a similar communion of love. A community in which we find our lives as we lose them on behalf of God and others. Our *imago Dei* certainly includes our individuality, but it does not end there. While we are each an image bearer, we better reflect God together in loving community. This is what we were created for. But sin makes it hard for us to trust each other, and when we do, we let each other down. This is no reason to give up on life, though. The

Jesus Way is about modeling God's abundant life on behalf of everybody, because in Jesus it is available to anybody.

Paradoxically, we become ourselves only as we transcend ourselves—we find our identity with God and others through sacrificial love, which requires that we let go of our lives. And this has to be chosen freely. Sacrifice is not love when it is demanded of us. The Trinity is indeed the model for unity in diversity and for individuality within community. The paradoxical nature of the Trinity—God is one (unity) and God is three (diversity)—solves our social dilemmas. God being one and God being three is contradictory at one level, but at a higher level, they define each other. The one is the three, and the three are the one.

Yet the Trinity helps us only inasmuch as we live into it! The idea of the Trinity is not enough; we need to be the image of God in the world. All the social problems in the world, despite being incredibly complex, boil down to a failure to love others as God loves. This is why Jesus commands us to love each other just as he loved us (John 13:34-35). Following Jesus is not just about an eternity with God after we die; it is also about loving like Jesus so that we can have life here and now.

The paradoxical nature of the Trinity offers solutions to our social issues, and the paradoxical nature of Jesus as fully God and fully human offers solutions to our theological issues. Theologians sometimes argue over things like human free will versus God's foreknowledge, or God's separation from us in eternity versus God's presence with us in time. It can seem like we have to choose between two opposing things. It all boils down to whether we are comfortable with the paradox that Jesus reveals. When we are not comfortable with the paradox Jesus reveals, it looks like this:

Figure 1. Theology without the Jesus paradox

God		God
Divine Jesus		Human Jesus
God's being	versus	God's becoming
God's foreknowledge		Human free will
God's separation from us		God's presence with us

Yet all these issues become non-issues when we embrace that Jesus is simultaneously fully God and fully human. His divinity demands everything on the left side of the chart, and his humanity demands everything on the right side of the chart. They are different, but they come together as one in Christ. Just as Father, Son, and Spirit are distinguishable (three persons) yet inseparable (one being), so the divine and human natures of Jesus are distinguishable (two natures) yet inseparable (one person). At a lower level these ideas seem to contradict, but at a higher level they define each other as a single, if paradoxical, thing. They are two sides of the same coin, even if we can only see one side at a time.

Figure 2. Theology with the Jesus paradox

God beyond time		God within time
Divine Jesus		Human Jesus
God's being	*and*	God's becoming
God's foreknowledge		Human free will
God's separation from us		God's presence with us

The first two ecumenical councils in the fourth century did not clear up every question. Once the full divinity of the Son and Spirit was settled, the question moved to how Jesus can be both God and human. In the fifth century, some began to wonder if Jesus is perhaps half God and half human, or maybe two people—one human and one divine. At the third and fourth ecumenical councils in Ephesus (431) and Chalcedon (451), it was agreed that Jesus is not two persons, nor is he half human or half divine. He is one person with two natures. Jesus is fully God, but he has taken on the fullness of humanity without ceasing to be God.

Theologians call this the **hypostatic union**. *Hypostatic* comes from the Greek *hypostasis,* which means "foundational being." Hebrews 1:3 contains the word: "[The Son] is the reflection of God's glory and the exact imprint of God's *hypostasis* [foundational being]." The councils defined the hypostatic union to mean that the foundational being of both God and humanity existed in the single person of Jesus. Jesus' humanity and divinity are *perfectly distinguishable* in that he has two different natures. Yet his divinity and humanity are *totally inseparable* in that they both cohere in his singular person.

This is abstract, philosophical language that requires an embrace of paradox. Yet it matters for us because it means that in Jesus, God and humanity are eternally joined. God and humanity are not the same, nor are they haphazardly mixed, but in Christ Jesus they come together as one in him. Jesus is indeed our foundation. God has chosen out of love to never let humanity go—he has eternally become human! The Son becomes for us *the way, the truth, and the life.* The hypostatic union expresses that in Jesus the foundational being of God and the foundational being of humanity are eternally linked. Wow. This is why eternal life is found through the faith of Jesus for us, and our faith in Jesus.

While Jesus is the ultimate walking paradox, we too are walking paradoxes. Our individualism seems to run against a united community. Yet at a deeper level, we find that there is no community without individuals, and all individuals owe their life to a community. The community that the Trinity demon-strates was a primary reason why some early Anabaptists freely shared resources with each other and in some cases held all property and possessions in common. Peter Riedemann, a founder of the Hutterite Brethren, wrote from prison in 1540: "Community means that those who have this fellowship hold all things in common, no one having anything for oneself, but each sharing all things with the others. Just so, the Father has nothing for himself, but everything he has, he has with the Son. Likewise, the Son has nothing for himself, but all he has, he has with the Father and with all who have fellowship with him."[1]

The being of the Trinity is the communion of the three per-sons. As God's image, the being of humanity is, ideally, all of us together. We adequately bear God's image when humanity is in loving community. The *imago Dei* is a plural image. It is the communion of male and female together, or as Gene-sis 1:26-27 puts it, "'Let us [God] make humankind in our image. . . .' In the image of God he created them; male and female he created them."

Like Jesus, we are to live sacrificially on behalf of each other. Like Jesus, we are to hold loosely on to our possessions and even our lives. Jesus is our guide in this, because Jesus is our God, as well as our fellow human example. His body was bro-ken for us, and his blood was poured out for us. We remember, proclaim, and celebrate this whenever we eat the bread and drink the cup of communion. Like the first Christ-followers, when we share in the Lord's Supper we are reminded that we are one in Jesus. His body was broken apart so that we could be united in him. His lifeblood was poured out so that we could be filled with divine life.

Our life is not just our own, because that is not how life happens. The wheat of the bread and the grapes of the cup had to die in order to nourish our life. Jesus had to die to give us eternal life. As we give to God and others, we receive from God and others. The water of life flows in and out. We breathe in and we breathe out. Life is never grasped on to individually, it is given and received only between persons. This is how we bear God's image together, as persons in loving community.

4

Why Does Jesus, Above All Else, Reveal God to Us?

In the beginning was the Word, and the Word was with God, and the Word was God. . . . No one has ever seen God, but the one and only Son, who is himself God, and is in closest relationship with the Father, has made him known.
—John 1:1, 18 (NIV)

Let's dig down to solid bedrock and talk specifically about Jesus. Hebrews 1:3 says that "[the Son] is the reflection of God's glory and the exact imprint of God's very being." Colossians 1 tells us that "he is the image of the invisible God" (v. 15) and that "in him all the fullness of God was pleased to dwell" (v. 19). Jesus is the perfect revelation of God to us. Of course he is not the most important member of the Trinity—all three are equally God. Yet he is the only divine person who became human. In doing so he perfectly demonstrated what God is like as well as how we should live. Jesus reveals the character of God and how we should pattern our lives.

Paradoxically, when we see one person of the Trinity, we always see the other two, for they are one. This means that if we are ever lacking one person, then we are lacking the other two as well! They are always one in being and one in action. Because they are one in being, there is no ladder or chain of being among them. Because they are one in action, there is no ladder or chain of command among them.[1] They are one in love. Jesus said that to see him was to have seen the Father (John 14:9). And Scripture teaches us that when we experience the Holy Spirit, we experience Jesus, even while Jesus was led by and empowered by the Spirit. One divine person never acts apart from the others. Jesus said that he does nothing apart from the Father (John 5:19), and he did nothing apart from the Spirit.

We will take a closer look at this divine community in the next chapter. For now it is enough to focus on something unique about the Son. Among the Father, Son, and Spirit, only the Son became human. And this becomes our bedrock, for we humans desperately need a God we can relate to. Jesus literally makes relationship with God a reality for us.

We cannot understand Jesus apart from the Trinity, nor can we understand the Trinity apart from Jesus. Everyone likes their idea of who Jesus is, but not everyone likes Jesus' own idea of who he is. Accepting Jesus' self-identity as both God and human is essential for relationship. Someone might think that I'm a good teacher, but if they can't accept that I am also married to my wife, then I don't see how our relationship can move forward. We can think great things of Jesus, but if we can't accept that he is who he says he is, then we are not yet open to the truth that Jesus reveals.

As God, Jesus is one being with the Trinity, and as a human, Jesus is one of us. This is fantastic in every sense of the word. It is a stumbling block for some and foolishness to others. It is the way to eternal life. The paradox of the Trinity makes sense only in light of the paradox of Jesus being both God and human. This is why we should cross-link the two paradoxes. It gives us a fuller picture of who God is as Trinity. Since Jesus understood them together, it helps when we do as well.

Figure 3. The double paradox

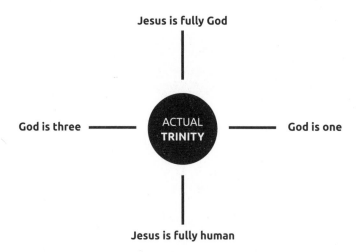

When we hold both paradoxes in tension, we stay centered in our understanding of God according to Jesus. The paradox of the one and the three matters because it is the only way God can be love: a community of persons who give and receive life freely and mutually. The paradox of Jesus being God and human matters because in Jesus, God chooses to be eternally linked to humanity, offering us eternal life. When we fail to hold the tension, we stray from the center and end up on what I call "the outer rim." The outer rim is where all our non-trinitarian views live. Most of us are partial to one or more of these anti-trinitarian views. We might even find these views taught in church from time to time.

Figure 4. The double paradox with the outer rim

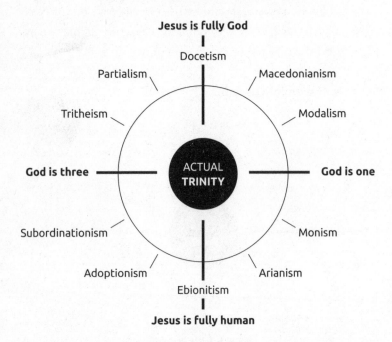

In case you are curious, below are the definitions of the ten views on the outer rim, starting on the lower right of the diagram and going clockwise. Each is a result of overemphasizing the truth of one side of the paradox to the exclusion of the truth of the other side. I encourage you to think about which of these views you are partial to, and why.

- **Monism** – There is no Trinity, just a single divine person who is God.

- **Arianism** – Jesus is more than human, yet he is created by the Father and is less than fully God.
- **Ebionitism** – While special, Jesus is not divine; he is only human.
- **Adoptionism** – Jesus was born human and was never divine, but he was adopted by God and granted divinity by God.
- **Subordinationism** – One or two persons of the Trinity are somehow less divine, or permanently ordered under the other persons.
- **Tritheism** – There are three separate Gods of Father, Son, and Holy Spirit.
- **Partialism** – Each person of the Trinity is only partially God.
- **Docetism** – Jesus is only divine and not human; he merely appeared to be human.
- **Macedonianism** – The Holy Spirit is created and not really God like the Father and Son.
- **Modalism** – God is one person only, with three distinct modes of being or expressions in history.

We like the outer rim because we can get rid of paradoxes that make us uncomfortable. On the outer rim Jesus is just human, or just God, or something in between, but not both. God can be one, or God can be many, but not both. God can be separate from us, or God can be near to us, but not both. The God that Jesus reveals is often too fantastic to accept. A God of unity in diversity, a God of interpersonal love, and an eternal God who has freely chosen an eternity with us. This is the God that Jesus reveals, and it makes even Christians squirm. A lonely-person God is easier to handle, for a God of abstract transcendence cannot be personal love, and cannot expect personal love from us in return.

Avoiding the rim and learning to hold the tension of the Trinity is like learning to ride a bike. When you get on a bike for the very first time and put your feet on the pedals, you start to fall to one side or the other. It is only natural. There is a knife's edge of balance that is difficult to find. In time you learn that balance is achievable, and made much easier as you get moving. Movement is key. As you push on the pedals, you begin to work through the imbalance. You constantly adjust left to right and back again to keep from falling. And the more you work through it with movement, the sturdier you become. Faith in the Trinity is similar; as we put it to use in our lives, we find balance easier to attain. In time, the constant adjustment from one side to the other can become automatic.

Yet if we find that we are constantly falling off to one side or another, there is a remedy. Remember that the Trinity is two paradoxes, not one. If we find ourselves out of balance in one paradox, then we can use the other paradox as a set of training wheels. In our diagram, one paradox intersects the other. If you are out of whack with one paradox, see if you are in balance with the other. Like training wheels, an aid for not falling to the left or the right will also help us to not fall forward or backward.

This is important because we have a lot of selfish reasons to take a position on the outer rim. The Jesus Way is demanding, because love is demanding. If God really is one and three and Jesus really is God and human, then we are unable to wiggle out of Jesus' commands to love as he loves. It is more convenient to take an unbalanced position, removing either Jesus' divinity or his humanity. The result either way is that we remove his lordship in our lives.

I am sad to see Christianity in North America broken down into two camps, both based on incomplete views of

Jesus. On the left are those who follow Jesus as teacher, but not as savior. He becomes merely our example of how we all can live a godly life. His nature as the eternal God who is entirely different from us is downplayed. Jesus is just an example of the divine potential in all of us. When Jesus becomes our teacher but not our savior, we are left to save ourselves. It is tempting to think that we can follow Jesus' example yet be our own saviors, but history has shown that we are ill equipped to save ourselves.

Yet on the right are those who praise Jesus as savior. Salvation is only found through him, they rightly say. But even here many are uncomfortable with his paradoxical nature, so we think of him as less than the Father and not really God. Again, his full divinity is downplayed. Jesus is just a transaction or a middleman—kind of God, but not really God; kind of human, but not really human. And so after we accept his salvation we do not submit ourselves to his teaching above all other teachings. We largely do what we want, maintain allegiances to other things, and then cherry-pick Scripture that justifies our selfish interests. When Jesus is just our savior but not our teacher, we are left to teach ourselves, and we inevitably conform to the world around us.

While the Anabaptist tradition certainly has its practitioners on the left and right, it generally offers a third way. In the great commission, as Jesus tells his followers to baptize in the name of the Father, Son, and Holy Spirit, he says to "[teach] them to obey everything that I have commanded you" (Matthew 28:20). When we combine obedience to Jesus' teaching on how we should live (Jesus as our teacher) with obedience to Jesus' teachings on who he is as God and human (Jesus as our savior), we arrive at a fuller discipleship in which Jesus is our Lord. As our Lord he is our authority in both what we believe and how we behave. When Jesus is our Lord, we belong to him completely, and he becomes our teacher and our savior as well.

Only when we accept Jesus for who he says he is and not our ideal version can he challenge us and, through his Spirit, transform us. When we submit to Jesus we become one of his disciples. To be *a disciple* literally means to be *a learner*. As we learn from Jesus, we put his way of love into practice. We obey his command to love each other as he loved us, which is the way the Trinity loves. When we give our lives to Jesus, he promises that the Holy Spirit begins to live within us. The Spirit deserves a few chapters of his own, but this book does not have the space. The Spirit does not mind—the Spirit's joy is to always point us to Jesus.[2] In 1 Corinthians 12:3, Paul says that "no one can say 'Jesus is Lord' except by the Holy Spirit." Just as the Son points to the Father, so too the Spirit points to the Son. The three persons are always one. They are a package deal.

Since the three are one God, we are free to address either one or all three when we pray. Christians usually pray to the Father, because this is how Jesus taught us to pray. Like Jesus, we pray in Jesus, by the Holy Spirit, to the Father. The Son came alongside us as a human, and the Spirit now indwells humanity, yet the Father remains wholly transcendent beyond us. Therefore, the Son and Spirit serve as mediators when we pray. This should not be an excuse, however, to exclude Jesus and the Spirit from our prayers. God is one being, so talking to the Son and Spirit when we pray means that we are also talking to the Father. The three are one, and all three are involved in everything that God does. There are no secrets between them. It is difficult to build relationships with the Son and Spirit without including them when we pray. Prayer, like all life, involves the Father beyond us, the Spirit within us, and Jesus beside us.

They are one, yet each of the three delights to relate to us uniquely while always pointing us to the others. This is a reflection of God's own communion, where they relate to each other uniquely and direct their love toward one another. When we follow Jesus as Lord, teacher, and savior, then we better come to know the entire Trinity as the one God of love. As 1 John 4:9 says, "God's love was revealed among us in this way: God sent his only Son into the world so that we might live through him." If we want to know what God is like, we look to Jesus. We model our lives after him. Jesus is the revelation of God in full. And because only Jesus is both God and human, only Jesus eliminates the separation between ourselves and God.

5

How Is God Perfectly One, Yet Perfectly Three?

You know [the spirit], because he abides with you, and he will be in you. . . . On that day you will know that I am in my Father, and you in me, and I in you.
—John 14:17, 20

I like to watch the group dance acts on the show *America's Got Talent*. It could have something to do with the fact that I am the last person around who could ever perform in such an act. Yet it is also because I see a picture of trinitarian love in these group dances. In any communal dance, there are the individual dancers, but when they work together in unison something wonderful happens. Rather than a bunch of people doing their own routines next to each other, their work can combine to form a single, dynamic, and often captivating work of art.

God is interpersonal love, and love requires persons who give and receive it. Love requires action or movement from each individual, as well as harmonized movement from the whole community. This fluid giving and receiving of life and love between the divine persons has long been thought of in terms of a dance.

Perichoresis is the theological word that describes the life and love of the communal God. It was a word used by early church leaders to describe Jesus' paradoxical humanity and divinity, as well as the paradoxical interanimation of the three persons of the Trinity that we see in the Bible. *Perichoresis* seems to derive from the Greek roots *peri* (around) and *chorein* (to give away or to make space). *Chorein* is also the origin of the English word *choreography*. Perichoresis describes the divine dance of self-giving love that is the triune God. In this dance, each member pours himself out into the others, even as he is filled by the others. They interanimate and interpenetrate each other so completely that they are one perfect essence— one mind, one will, one work . . . one being.

Perichoresis was used by the early church to refute Arianism in the fourth century (Arianism being the belief that the Son is created by the Father and is not really God). John of Damascus formalized perichoresis as a doctrine in the eighth century, and it has remained a core idea in Eastern Christianity (the Orthodox Churches) ever since. Sadly, the Western churches (Catholic and Protestant) didn't speak Greek, so the term was lost to them as they separated from the East. Amazingly, the idea of perichoresis (if not the word) sprung up again in the West during the Reformation, when early Anabaptist leaders began talking and writing about the Trinity as a unity in which everything is shared—a communion of mutuality, interdependence, and reciprocity.[1] Despite having no interaction at all with Eastern Orthodox Christianity, these Radical Reformers sounded a lot like Orthodox Christians, yet their notions came exclusively from Scripture.

This perichoretic dance is an eternal movement in which Father, Son, and Spirit lovingly submit to each other, even as each is empowered by each other. In their one perfect being, the three are each their unique selves as they surrender to and enliven each other. While this is an eternal movement *outside of creation*, we know about it because we have seen it characterized by God *within creation*. It overflows to us in the acts of creating, redeeming, and restoring the world. Scripture reveals to us that the work of the Trinity in the world is the same eternal dance of the Trinity beyond time. Imagine it with me.[2]

ETERNITY

Imagine a God who exists eternally as a community of three equally divine persons. The communion of the three is so perfect that they are one divine being. And this one relational God is love. This love is dynamic—open to the other, to giving and receiving. Each divine person exists in and through this love. Each pours himself out sacrificially on behalf of the other two, even as he is filled by the other two. The one is the three, while the three are the one. This is the eternal dance of love.

CREATION

Now imagine that God chooses to extend this love beyond Godself, to overflow it into something new. So God creates the universe. In an act of self-limitation and sacrifice, God pulls back to make room for something other than God. The Spirit takes the lead in the eternal dance and hovers over the primordial "waters" of this void. The Spirit then pours himself out into the Father and the Son, overflowing the eternal dance of love into creation. Through his self-emptying, the Spirit sends the Father as Creator and gives divine power over our creation to the Son, through whom all things are created. And it was good.

Then God said, "Let *us* make humankind in *our* image, according to *our* likeness" (Genesis 1:26, italics mine). Male and female, individuals created in the image of the one God, yet together created in the image of the communal God who exists through interpersonal relationships. And it was very good. Yet there were bound to be problems for a Creator who is love, for love requires persons who are free to accept or reject their part in the dance, persons who are free to choose for or against relationship. And so the relational barrier of sin and death infects us, separating humanity from God. Yet from eternity the Trinity had chosen a solution to our problem. A solution with a great cost.

REDEMPTION

Imagine that the Father takes the lead in the eternal dance. Reciprocating the work of the Spirit, he pours himself out into the Son and Spirit, the dance of love overflowing. In self-emptying, the Father sends the Son as Redeemer and gives divine power over our redemption to the Spirit. The Son temporarily gives up his divine privileges and becomes fully human. God submits to becoming a part of creation, yet God cannot stop being God. He takes on our fallen humanity—a humanity that can sin as we do—but through obedience to the Father and submission to the Spirit, Jesus does not sin like us, making a way for us. In Jesus, God is perfectly represented for us, and the character of God is fully seen in his submitted, self-giving, Spirit-empowered life.

God makes space within eternity for humanity, for God and humanity exist perfectly and paradoxically together in the person of Jesus Christ. Now watch how sin and its curse—our suffering, alienation, even death itself—is taken upon himself by Jesus on the cross, causing him to experience a loss of communion with the Father and the Spirit. He feels abandoned. "Why have you forsaken me?" he cries, echoing the lament of Psalm 22. Yet Jesus does not reject his humanity—he knows the psalm ends in the good and perfect peace between God and us. The Spirit empowers him to be faithful to the end.

God pours Godself out for us, and takes the consequences of sin and death upon himself. As Jesus speaks his last words, he commends his spirit into the arms of God. And then he takes his last, dying breath. The dance seems to end abruptly. It is hard to imagine. Yet the Father and Spirit do not let go of their beloved, for the being of God cannot be broken. What is the Trinity to do when Jesus dies? What they always do, and had purposed to do all along—they dance. God makes space for humanity as Jesus extends the dance straight through sin, suffering, and death.

Jesus never lets humanity go, and Father and Spirit never let Jesus go. Jesus is one with us and one with Father and Spirit. Thus God holds on to us through death itself. The Trinity reaches through the very core of darkness, and there Jesus falls in complete trust into the embrace of Father and Spirit. And the Trinity dances, this time on both sides of the relational barrier, and this dance shatters sin and death, raising Jesus from the dead. And so begins the good and perfect peace of a new creation.

RESTORATION

Imagine now that the risen Son reciprocates, taking the lead in the eternal dance. All authority in heaven and on earth has been given to him, so he pours himself out into the Spirit and the Father, the dance of love overflowing. In doing so he sends the Spirit as our Restorer, who is actively preparing the world for Jesus' return. Jesus waits for the time when all things will be reconciled to God, when he will give all things back to the Father. And the Father, who knows the day of final restoration, works, and waits, and loves.

The powers of evil and death have suffered a mortal blow. We can live through our own suffering and death knowing that like Christ's suffering and death, it will end in total victory and reunion with our beloved God. Soon the day will come when time and space will be folded into eternity. For those who say yes to God, the dance draws us in. For in Jesus—who holds both divine and human, eternal and temporal, heaven and earth, perfectly and paradoxically together—the dance has been extended to you and to me. Jesus reaches out his hand and asks us to follow him, desiring us to join this eternal movement of love, or what he simply calls "eternal life."

In this light, God can be nothing other than perfectly one, yet perfectly three.

Figure 5. Perichoresis, the dance of the Trinity

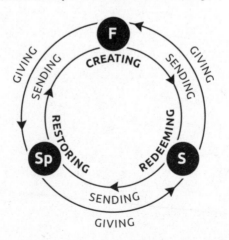

6

Why Isn't the Father Alone Really God?

You know that among the Gentiles those whom they recognize as their rulers lord it over them, and their great ones are tyrants over them. But it is not so among you; but whoever wishes to become great among you must be your servant, and whoever wishes to be first among you must be slave of all. For the Son of Man came not to be served but to serve, and to give his life a ransom for many.
—Mark 10:42-45

I can't think of anything more humbling than feet. It's awkward even writing about them. They are always on the ground, getting dirty, or covered up, getting sweaty. And feet were a lot worse for wear during Jesus' time. When people came in for the day, their feet needed to be washed, a task reserved for the lowest person in the household. In John 13, as

Jesus began his last night with his disciples, he took the lowest place and washed their feet. Jesus was their Lord and God, yet he did the lowliest of tasks. Then he told them,

> Do you know what I have done to you? You call me Teacher and Lord—and you are right, for that is what I am. So if I, your Lord and Teacher, have washed your feet, you also ought to wash one another's feet. For I have set you an example, that you also should do as I have done to you. Very truly, I tell you, servants are not greater than their master, nor are messengers greater than the one who sent them. (John 13:12-16)

The picture of love in the last chapter took us through the entire biblical narrative, from the first chapter of Genesis to the last chapter of Revelation. You might be thinking, "Well that's a nice picture, but isn't there a lot of Scripture which points to the supremacy of the Father?" Or, "When push comes to shove, isn't the Father alone really God?" The short answer to both questions is no. The passages that might imply a lesser status of the Son or the Spirit (or both) speak to the mutual submission within the Trinity, or to the humility of the Spirit in always pointing to the Son, or to the Son giving up his divine privileges, temporarily, for his earthly ministry as a human. During Jesus' ministry he embodied perfect obedience to God as an example for all of humanity to follow. Eternally speaking, the Trinity is a perfect communion of love in which their loving unity does not require obedience.

Jesus washed his disciples' feet, yet this did not make him less than them. Now, in the eyes of the world it certainly would communicate that Jesus is less than the disciples. Only people who are lesser serve, one would think. This is precisely why Jesus washed their feet, and why he tells us to wash one another's feet. Jesus is demonstrating that being greater, and that being God, involves humble service, not just power and leadership. For God, service and leadership are one and the same. The humbling of Jesus does not prove his inferiority, but his superiority. His humility as a human before the Father does not reveal him to be less than the Father.

God is love, and divine love requires a community of persons who give and receive life freely and mutually. Every act of love must be chosen freely in order to be love, otherwise it is just forced or robotic action. If the Son and Spirit are inferior to the Father and must simply obey him, then they would not reveal a communal God of love, but something else entirely. The Father, Son, and Spirit serve each other in freedom and equality. They give of themselves so completely that they are one. This is not how humans tend to do things. We want everybody to "know their place"; we conform to social hierarchies of lording over each other, and we want others to do what we see as best from our own selfish perspectives.

While every true act of love requires freedom, I concede that not every act of love requires equality and reciprocity. God loves us, and we are not equal to God, and we are free to not reciprocate God's love. And of course we do not always reciprocate each other's love. Yet our refusal to reciprocate love does not make the love offered any less. Our refusal to reciprocate God's love does not make God any less God, nor does our refusal to reciprocate a fellow human's love make the one who gave such love any less human. It simply means that in our refusal to love, we become less human, for love is what we are created for.

The eternal communion of love that is the Trinity absolutely requires equality and reciprocity. If a person of the Trinity is less essential to divine love, which is what God is, then that person simply is not essentially God. If one is not essentially

God, then one is not God at all. In the Jesus Way, there is God and there is not God, but there is no semi-God, demi-God, hemi-God, or quasi-God. God is love, and therefore Father, Son, and Holy Spirit are each and equally the God who is love.

I encourage Christians to stop thinking like Arians. The Son and Spirit are not bridge beings—middlemen who are a little lower than God and a little higher than us. They are either God or they are not. And if they are not God, then their love is just the limited version of love that characterizes human society. The Trinity does not reflect our fallen, hierarchical relations. People often use a false idea of the Trinity to justify lording over each other, but this is simply us projecting our own disordered version of community back onto God. This gets things exactly wrong. God does not reflect our fallen humanity. When we project a false view of God to justify our selfish misbehavior, we lose God. Jesus and the Spirit are not slaves or robots who simply follow the Father's commands. If God is one being, then Father, Son, and Spirit are of one will, and they make decisions in love, as one. We were created to reflect this divine image of communion in our lives together.

Jesus did freely submit himself to becoming human, in which he had to fully rely on the Spirit and be fully obedient to the Father. In this way he perfectly modeled for us how we should live in relation to the Spirit and the Father. In John 14:28, Jesus said that "the Father is greater than I." He was saying this as someone who had given up divine privileges in order to be authentically human. Hebrews 5:8 says that "although he was a Son, he learned obedience through what he suffered." Since during his ministry Jesus had to *learn* obedience to the Father, we know that this was something brand new to Jesus. He was always equal to the Father as God, yet he had to learn obedience as a human, and he modeled it perfectly for us.[1]

Paul describes this in his letter to the Philippians, in which he quotes a very early Christian hymn:

> In your relationships with one another, have the same mindset as Christ Jesus:
>
> Who, being in very nature God,
>   did not consider equality with God something to be
>   used to his own advantage;
> rather, he made himself nothing
>   by taking the very nature of a servant,
>   being made in human likeness.
> And being found in appearance as a man,
>   he humbled himself
>   by becoming obedient to death—
>   even death on a cross!
>
> Therefore God exalted him to the highest place
>   and gave him the name that is above every name,
> that at the name of Jesus every knee should bow,
>   in heaven and on earth and under the earth,
> and every tongue acknowledge that Jesus Christ is Lord,
>   to the glory of God the Father. (Philippians 2:5-11 NIV)

Jesus is a different kind of lord than the lords among us humans. As the passage from Mark 10 at the top of this chapter states, humans with power lord it over others and become tyrants over others. This is the world under Satan's influence. Jesus, however, is a lord who serves. He gave up everything in order to give us everything. And Jesus is a different kind of lord because he is a different kind of God. He reveals that God is a God who freely pours out love. Since Jesus perfectly reveals the character of the Father, we learn that God is a lord—the Lord—who serves in love. The essential command of Jesus is that we do the same.

Father, Son, and Spirit lift up one another and not themselves. Yet in doing so, each in turn is lifted up by the others.

The three are one in love. We see this within Scripture in their action in the world. The Father is our creator, but it is the Spirit who initiates creation (Genesis 1:2), and it is the Son through whom the Father created all things (John 1:3; Colossians 1:17). The Son is our redeemer, but it is the Father who initiates redemption (John 3:16), and it is the Spirit through whom the Son redeems us. The Spirit is our restorer, but it is the Son who initiates our restoration (John 15:26; 16:7; 20:21-23), and it is the Father through whom we are restored (John 14–16; Acts 1:7; 2:33). You see, in one divine person we always see the other two, acting in and for each other, and for the world as well. They are always three, yet one. And while the world is not part of the Trinity, God has chosen to include the world in the life of the Trinity.

Figure 6. The Trinity and us

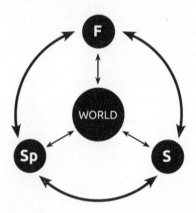

Father, Son, and Spirit are each Lord, but they serve rather than lord over each other. Jesus is our Lord, but he serves rather than lords over us. We also must not lord over each other if we want to live the Jesus Way. The great commission begins with Jesus saying that "all authority in heaven and on earth has been given to me" (Matthew 28:18). The Father has given everything to the resurrected Son, even all the authority of heaven. We learn later in Scripture (1 Corinthians 15) that the Son will gladly give it all back to the Spirit and the Father at the end of time. The kingdom of God looks entirely different from the kingdoms of this world. If Jesus reveals who God is, then mutual submission in love is who God is. In God's kingdom, service and leadership are the same. This servant leadership can be embodied a thousand different ways, but it is always something like washing each other's feet.

7

What Does the Trinity Say about Gender, Hierarchy, and Roles?

I give you a new commandment, that you love one another. Just as I have loved you, you also should love one another. By this everyone will know that you are my disciples, if you have love for one another.
—John 13:34-35

How should we all live together and organize our communities? Since the Trinity is foundational, what we think about it matters, but we often cannot agree on who God is. We tend to take our preferences on what perfect humanity should be and then project that onto God, making God in our own image. For example, if we think that perfect humanity is white and male, then we will think of God as white and male as well. Those in power like our racial hierarchies, our gender hierarchies, and our economic hierarchies. We especially like the broken image of lording over each other, inherited from the fall. This is just as God predicted when he told Eve that because of the fall, Adam would rule over her, even as she sought to control him.

Jesus rescues us from the trap of arguing about who should lord over whom. Rather than making our own gods in our own image, we have been given God's exact image in Jesus (Colossians 1:15; Hebrews 1:3). This is why Jesus alone is our Lord, teacher, and savior. With Jesus we no longer have to guess what God is like. God is like Jesus, so we should model everything on the way of Jesus. As people created in God's image, we should reflect what the Trinity demonstrates about gender, hierarchy, and roles. Of course we need to remember that a human person is not the same as a divine person. We do not transcend sex, gender, and culture as God does. So what principles can we learn from the Trinity that apply to Christian society? I break it down to four principles:

1. God is not sexed or gendered—God transcends human sex and gender. Therefore, gender-inclusive language for God is permissible, even welcome, as long as we do not lose our anchor in the primary titles of Father, Son, and Holy Spirit. The Bible is full of female images for God, so using female images for God gives us a more complete picture of the God whose image we bear. For example, when we refer to God as our Mother alongside the idea that God is our Father, we get a more accurate and complete picture. The Spirit is referred to as *she* in the Old Testament, and is given a gender-neutral treatment in the New Testament. Jesus as a human is of course male, but even he transcends gender to include all people.

Every biblical reference to the incarnation of Jesus speaks explicitly of the Son becoming *human* as opposed to becoming a man.[1] It is remarkable that the texts which talk about

Jesus taking on human form take great '
human, and not as man or male, whe⌐   ⌐⌐ the Bible is
not concerned with gender-inclusive language. The New Testament writers, guided by the Spirit, took what were at the time
extraordinary measures to communicate that Jesus is a particular *human* (not *man*), representative of all people. Jesus does
not represent any one particular people group, but all of us
together. This is how he offers redemption to all of humanity.

2. No human sex or gender reflects God better than another.
Of course the biblical argument can be made that Adam was
created first, and that Eve was created out of Adam. This does
give Adam primacy, but we must balance that with the biblical
fact that Eve was created last, which signifies that she is the
apex of creation and in some way superior to Adam. After
all, the animals were created before Adam, and the order of
creation is from the lesser representation of God to the greater.
Also, Eve is created because Adam is severely lacking as a
human. The word we often translate as "helper" in Genesis
2:18 (ESV: "It is not good that the man should be alone, I
will make him a helper fit for him") is the same word used to
describe God in relationship to Israel. Woman is a helper to
man in a similar way that God is a helper to Israel.

The point is that male and female correspond to each
other, and that only together do they fully function as God's
image. When we wrongly think of God as a lone individual, it
becomes natural to assume that a certain race, class, or gender comes closer to God than another. The Christian view is
that God is a community of diversity. All races, classes, and
genders reflect God equally. There is neither Jew nor Greek,
slave nor free, male and female, for we are all one in Christ
(Galatians 3:28). As Paul describes in Romans 8, all of us, men
and women alike, can be adopted as "sons" (KJV) by God.

Paul here is not suggesting that women become men, but that men and women alike are children of God with full rights as God's heirs. This was something that daughters of the time did not enjoy, but while human daughters may not enjoy the privileges of human sons, in God's kingdom, daughters receive all the same privileges as sons.

3. The Trinity doesn't need permanent hierarchies, because they each give everything to each other in love. The ideal human society should strive for the same, in which no one person or group is worth more than another, and nobody demands submission by lording over any other. Jesus as a human submits to the Father and relies on the Spirit, and we are to model his example. Yet Philippians 2 and Hebrews 5:8 make clear that this humbling is a temporary condition for Jesus. The Son is not permanently ordered under the Father. If that were the case, then he would by definition lack something essential to divinity and there could be no Trinity at all.

While Jesus is fully God and fully human, we are neither God nor fully human. This is why we like hierarchies. We are all of us *equally* human, but because of sin we are not *fully* human. Our humanity—the *imago Dei*—is marred and lacks perfection. We are denatured by sin, dehumanized, which is why we lord over each other and have trouble living into mutual love. Yet the good news is that Jesus has come to remedy our inhuman situation. Jesus lives into full humanity on our behalf. We live into fuller humanity through faith in Jesus and by consenting to the transforming work of the Spirit within us. The Jesus Way is about living into Christ's resurrection victory over sin. This shows the world that mutual love—and a better humanity—is possible.

4. The Father, Son, and Spirit each take on roles in the economy of our salvation. We too will need to take on specific roles

in order to love the world. Father, Son, and Spirit are one, but they are not the same. We should strive to be one body, even while we celebrate that we are not the same. We need to take on roles in order to effectively love each other and the world. These roles should be based on our unique, God-given gifting and calling. Roles imply that sometimes some people lead, while others follow. Jesus reveals that for God, leadership and service are the same. We see this in the Trinity. Yet nothing about the Trinity itself implies that roles should be based on race or class, gender or sex. And nothing about the Trinity can excuse using the notion of roles to subjugate one group of people under another. Even in their roles, Father, Son, and Spirit are each always pointing to the other two persons. They are one, and they always act as one. In our roles, we should be loving the world, and celebrating and pointing to each other, not ourselves.

These four principles are not very specific. They do not tell us *precisely* how we should organize our churches. They do not lay out *exactly* the roles of pastors versus laypersons. They do not give us instructions that *perfectly* tell us how men and women should behave. What should we require of others? Who should do the laundry? When push comes to shove, who decides? We would all of us like the Trinity revealed in the Bible to give us the answer, but the answer the Trinity gives us is profoundly simple yet confoundingly complicated—perfect love. In perfect love, push never comes to shove, and never even comes to push. *The answer is precisely, exactly, and perfectly, love.* Love as defined by the love of God for us, revealed in Jesus.

A difficult but central teaching of Jesus is that everyone, even our enemy, is created in God's image. God's image is a communal image, and we bear God's image together. God is three, and God is also one. Humans are many, but in God's eyes, we are meant to be one. This is why Jesus tells us to pray for our enemies and never to return evil for evil. Jesus will someday return and make everything right in the world, but for now our job as Christ-followers is to love everyone as we have been loved by Jesus and to treat others as ourselves. In God's eyes, we are all deeply connected, and we are meant to experience better, deeper, and greater connection.

Jesus shows us that a life poured out for others leads to eternal life in God. Our calling is to sacrifice on behalf of others, especially those who are different from us. We are called to go out of our way to aid victims of violence, oppression, and poverty. Wherever we find ourselves, we take the lower place, and we lift up those at the bottom. In the Jesus Way, we pour out our lives as Jesus did. This does not mean that we simply become disposable to other people. Love must be freely chosen, or it is not love at all. Living sacrificially also does not mean that we aid or allow abuse of ourselves or others. Jesus did not just do what others wanted him to do. He did what was needed for the purposes of love. He died for it.

The hard part of the Jesus Way is that we must share in Jesus' death. We must go through it before we share in his resurrection. But in Jesus we are assured of resurrection. Therefore we have no fear of death! The first Jesus-followers gave up their lives so fearlessly that Christianity spread like crazy, against all odds. They used no coercion, and couldn't even if they had wanted to. There was something about them that people wanted in their life, even though it meant that they would likely be ostracized or killed. They had a hope that defied the ways of the world. It was worth everything. They found it through faith in Jesus Christ. It is a grace too good to be true. It is a life abounding with joy. It is the life of the Trinity, offered to us all. We live it by living the Jesus Way.

Glossary

adoptionism: The anti-trinitarian view that Jesus was only human and did not exist eternally as God the Son. However, the Father adopted Jesus as his Son and made him God.

Arianism: The anti-trinitarian view that the Son is created by the Father and is not really God. With Arianism, the Son is a middle-realm being between God and humanity.

Docetism: The anti-trinitarian view that the Son is not fully human and fully God. He is God only and merely appeared to become human.

Ebionitism: The anti-trinitarian view that while Jesus is the messiah, he is not God, but only human.

hypostatic union: Jesus is one person with two natures—fully God and fully human. Jesus is neither two people (one divine and one human), nor a mixture (half divine and half human). In Jesus the two natures do not mix, and remain distinguishable, yet they are joined together and are inseparable.

imago Dei: The image of God. We are created in this image. Since God is one yet many, so too we are meant to embody a single communion of love, made up of many individual persons. However, sin has distorted our image, making genuine community and individuality impossible apart from God.

incarnation: The eternal Son giving up divine privileges to become authentically human. His divine power during his earthly ministry did not come from the powers he temporarily set aside, but came from his union with the Father and the Spirit. While Jesus' earthly ministry was temporary, his incarnation was chosen by God from eternity, and is eternal. In Jesus, the Trinity has chosen to forever hold on to humanity, offering us eternal life.

Macedonianism: The anti-trinitarian view that the Holy Spirit is created by the Father, or by the Father and Son, and is not really God.

modalism: The anti-trinitarian view that God is one divine person with three modes, or three manifestations in history.

monism: The anti-trinitarian view that God is absolutely singular and is not a Trinity.

Nicene Creed: A creed that came from the first and second ecumenical councils. The statement of the first council, in Nicaea in the year 325, forms the nucleus of the creed and states that the Son is fully God and is one being with the

Father. The statement of the second council, in Constantinople in the year 381, adds the full divinity of the Holy Spirit. The full statement from 381 is the full Nicene Creed, also called the Niceno-Constantinopolitan Creed.

paradox: When two things are contradictory, but are both shown to be true anyway.

partialism: The anti-trinitarian view that Father, Son, and Spirit are not each fully God. They are each partially God, and together make up the full God.

perichoresis: The fluid interanimation and indwelling among Father, Son, and Spirit. They each empty themselves into each other. Yet as they pour themselves out in sacrificial love, they are each filled by the others. It is often thought of as a dance. It is how the church has thought of the Trinity paradoxically, as both one and three at the same time, with neither the three nor the one taking precedence. The one is the three, and the three are the one.

subordinationism: The anti-trinitarian view that the Son or Spirit or both are eternally less than, ordered under, or subordinated to the Father.

Trinity: God—one being in three persons—Father, Son, and Holy Spirit. The perfect love among the three persons constitutes the one being of God, and the one being of love constitutes the three divine persons. No person is permanently before or after, above or below another. They each freely submit to each other in love. In their mutual love they have one will and one character and are one in action. Yet they relate to each other in unique ways as Father, Son, and Spirit.

tritheism: The anti-trinitarian view that Father, Son, and Holy Spirit are three separate Gods, instead of the Trinity being one God.

YHWH: Four Hebrew letters associated with God that theologians call the tetragrammaton. When transliterated to English, the letter sequence sounds like YHWH, or Yahweh. We also get the word Jehovah (JHVH) from the same letters (people have not always agreed on what an ancient Hebrew consonant sounds like). YHWH is a form of shorthand for the name that God gives Moses, which means "I am who I am" or "I will be what I will be." Paradoxically, the name, by definition, is beyond naming.

Discussion and Reflection Questions

CHAPTER 1

1. How have you thought about God as Trinity? How has it mattered in your life, if at all?

2. If you are a Christian, how has following Jesus offered a unique perspective compared to other worldviews and religions?

3. Would you be any more or any less inspired to follow Jesus if he weren't fully God? How might a low view of Jesus be detrimental to your faith?

4. Do you have a high view of the Holy Spirit as a fully divine person who lives within you? What difference might it make in your life if this were the case, or if you believed it more?

CHAPTER 2

1. Are you comfortable with paradox in matters of faith? Do you think that paradox excuses contradictions, or has it made room for a deeper level of understanding?

2. If God is love, then what does that say about what love should look like for us?

3. The Trinity means that God is relational, and multi-personal at the core, yet most people (and most Christians) are accustomed to thinking of God as a "one-person" God. Do you prefer to think of God as one, or as three? Why do you think that is?

CHAPTER 3

1. Do you agree that love must be given freely (not coerced) in order to be love, and that it must be received freely? Why or why not? What does your view say about the nature of love?

2. Have you thought of the *imago Dei* as an individual image? Would your view of yourself as created in God's image change if the *imago Dei* is communal?

3. The hypostatic union means that Jesus' divinity and humanity are inseparable yet distinguishable, and it implies that in Jesus, God has chosen to be eternally linked to humanity. Discuss the implications of this theology.

CHAPTER 4

1. If we want to know what God is like, we look to Jesus. In your mind, is the character of the Father and the Holy Spirit identical to the character of Jesus? How do you see them as different?

2. Talk about the double paradox (see figure 3). Which of the two paradoxes is harder for you to accept? Why?

3. Look at the outer rim in figure 4. Where on the outer rim are you most prone to land? What do you think causes you to prefer this position?

4. Are you more likely to view Jesus as teacher or savior? What about your community or church? Do you think that your community has an appropriate balance?

CHAPTER 5

1. Was it helpful to imagine the life of the Trinity through the biblical story? How did it strike you, and what questions did it raise for you?

2. Perichoresis is the author's preferred metaphor for the Trinity. What metaphors for the Trinity do you like? What are their benefits and drawbacks?

CHAPTER 6

1. Are you convinced on the point that the Father is not more God than the Son or the Spirit? Why or why not?

2. If leadership and service are the same in God's eyes, how might that challenge leaders in your context? How might it challenge those who serve?

CHAPTER 7

1. We often can think that God looks a lot like us, or a lot like the powerful in society. What is your level of comfort when it comes to thinking of God beyond the attributes *white* and *male*?

2. That the Trinity is not a permanent hierarchy can be a controversial idea in Christianity. After reading this

book, what are your thoughts on God being three persons who are fully and equally God?

3. Do you agree with the four principles in this chapter? Does your community or church live as if they are true? How so?

4. Father, Son, and Holy Spirit each have taken on unique roles in our salvation, and they relate to each other uniquely, but always in love. We too are equal, yet we each have a unique calling. At this point in your life, what do you think God is calling you uniquely to do in the world?

Shared Convictions

Mennonite World Conference, a global community of Christian churches that facilitates community between Anabaptist-related churches, offers these shared convictions that characterize Anabaptist faith. For more on Anabaptism, go to ThirdWay.com.

By the grace of God, we seek to live and proclaim the good news of reconciliation in Jesus Christ. As part of the one body of Christ at all times and places, we hold the following to be central to our belief and practice:

1. God is known to us as Father, Son and Holy Spirit, the Creator who seeks to restore fallen humanity by calling a people to be faithful in fellowship, worship, service and witness.

2. Jesus is the Son of God. Through his life and teachings, his cross and resurrection, he showed us how to be faithful disciples, redeemed the world, and offers eternal life.

3. As a church, we are a community of those whom God's Spirit calls to turn from sin, acknowledge Jesus Christ as Lord, receive baptism upon confession of faith, and follow Christ in life.

4. As a faith community, we accept the Bible as our authority for faith and life, interpreting it together under Holy Spirit guidance, in the light of Jesus Christ, to discern God's will for our obedience.

5. The Spirit of Jesus empowers us to trust God in all areas of life so we become peacemakers who renounce violence, love our enemies, seek justice, and share our possessions with those in need.

6. We gather regularly to worship, to celebrate the Lord's Supper, and to hear the Word of God in a spirit of mutual accountability.

7. As a world-wide community of faith and life we transcend boundaries of nationality, race, class, gender and language. We seek to live in the world without conforming to the powers of evil, witnessing to God's grace by serving others, caring for creation, and inviting all people to know Jesus Christ as Saviour and Lord.

In these convictions we draw inspiration from Anabaptist forebears of the 16th century, who modelled radical discipleship to Jesus Christ. We seek to walk in his name by the power of the Holy Spirit, as we confidently await Christ's return and the final fulfillment of God's kingdom.

Adopted by Mennonite World Conference General Council, March 15, 2006

Notes

Introduction

  1 Michael Reeves, *Delighting in the Trinity: An Introduction to the Christian Faith* (Downers Grove, IL: IVP Academic, 2012). Read this book for an excellent case on why the Trinity is the most important aspect of Christian faith.

Chapter 2

  1 Thomas N. Finger, *A Contemporary Anabaptist Theology* (Downers Grove, IL: InterVarsity Press, 2004), 458.

  2 Bruxy Cavey, *(Re)union: The Good News of Jesus for Seekers, Saints, and Sinners* (Harrisonburg, VA: Herald Press, 2017), 25.

Chapter 3

  1 Peter Riedemann, *Peter Riedemann's Hutterite Confession of Faith*, ed. John Friesen (Scottdale, PA: Herald Press, 1999), 80.

Chapter 4

  1 Kevin Giles, *The Trinity and Subordinationism: The Doctrine of God and the Contemporary Gender Debate* (Downers Grove, IL: InterVarsity Press, 2002), 1–105.

  2 James Bryan Smith, *The Good and Beautiful God* (Downers Grove, IL: InterVarsity Press, 2009), 28.

Chapter 5

1 Thomas N. Finger, *A Contemporary Anabaptist Theology* (Downers Grove, IL: InterVarsity Press, 2004), 148–51, 454–64.

2 Steve Dancause, *Trinity Matters* (Carlisle, PA: Create Space/Steve Dancause, 2018), 22–25. What follows is a revised version of these pages from *Trinity Matters*.

Chapter 6

1 Gilbert Bilezikian, "Hermeneutical Bungee Jumping: Subordination in the Godhead," *Journal of the Evangelical Theological Society* 40, no. 1 (1997): 57–68.

Chapter 7

1 Stanley J. Grenz and Denise Muir Kjesbo, *Women in the Church: A Biblical Theology of Women in Ministry* (Downers Grove, IL: InterVarsity Press, 1995), 205–6.

The Author

Steve Dancause grew up in New Hampshire, where his family attended a small Baptist church. After working in biotechnology for several years after college, Steve went to seminary at The Seattle School of Theology and Psychology. It is there that he began wrestling with Christians' many questions about the Trinity and why it matters—questions he believes are worthy of a lifetime. Steve and his wife, Meredith, have one daughter. They currently live and pastor together in Sparks, Nevada.

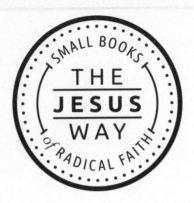

SMALL BOOKS
THE
JESUS
WAY
of **RADICAL FAITH**

HERALD
PRESS

www.HeraldPress.com. 1-800-245-7894